Destination Detectives

Italy

North America

Europe

Asia

ITALY

Africa

South America

Australasia

Paul Mason

Raintree

www.raintreepublishers.co.uk
Visit our website to find out more information about **Raintree** books.

To order:
☎ Phone 44 (0) 1865 888112
▤ Send a fax to 44 (0) 1865 314091
▭ Visit the Raintree Bookshop at **www.raintreepublishers.co.uk** to browse our catalogue and order online.

First published in Great Britain by
Raintree, Halley Court, Jordan Hill,
Oxford OX2 8EJ, part of Harcourt Education.
Raintree is a registered trademark of Harcourt
Education Ltd.

Produced for Raintree Publishers by Discovery Books Ltd
Editorial: Kathryn Walker, Melanie Copland, and Lucy Beevor
Design: Victoria Bevan, Rob Norridge, and Kamae Design
Picture Research: Hannah Taylor and Kay Alwegg
Production: Duncan Gilbert
Originated by Modern Age
Printed and bound in China
by South China Printing Company

10 digit ISBN 1 406 20402 1 (hardback)
13 digit ISBN 978 1 406 20402 5
10 09 08 07 06
10 9 8 7 6 5 4 3 2 1

10 digit ISBN 1 406 20409 9 (paperback)
13 digit ISBN 978 1 406 20409 4
10 09 08 07 06
10 9 8 7 6 5 4 3 2 1

British Library Cataloguing in Publication Data
Mason, Paul
Italy. – (Destination Detectives)
945'.093
A full catalogue record for this book is available from
the British Library.

This levelled text is a version of *Freestyle:
Destination Detectives: Italy*

Acknowledgements
Action Plus p. 22 (Neil Tingle); Alamy Images p. 20, pp.
18–19 (Andre Jenny), 38 (Chuck Pefley), 31 (David
Kilpatrick), 26 (Frank Chmura), 42 (Gareth McCormack),
17 (Image Source), 6b (Jon Arnold Images), 24 (Michael
Juno), pp. 14–15, 30 (PCL), 12 (westend61); Bridgeman Art
Library pp. 10–11, pp. 8–9 (Private Collection); Corbis pp.
36 (Alinari Archives), 11 (Archivo Iconografico S. A.), 29
(Free Agents Limited), 37 (K. M. Westermann), 21 (Owen
Franken), 4-5 (Ted Spiegel), 23 (Tim De Waele), 43b (Vince
Streano); Corbis Royalty Free p. 15; Corbis Sygma p. 43t
(Alfio Scigliano); Fototeca ENIT pp. 5, 6m, 39, 41b; Getty
Images pp. 12–13 (Stone), 18 (The Image Bank), 9
(PhotoDisc); Harcourt Education Ltd pp. 6t, 16, 27, 34, 35,
40, 41t (Sharron Lovell); JNTO p. 13; Rail Images p. 32r;
Rex Features pp. 28 (Canlo Romaniello), 25 (SIPA Press);
thirdangle.com pp. 32l.

Cover photograph of gondolas in Venice reproduced with
permission of Alamy Images/Eyebyte.

Every effort has been made to contact copyright
holders of any material reproduced in this book.
Any omissions will be rectified in subsequent
printings if notice is given to the publishers.

The paper used to print this book comes from
sustainable resources.

Disclaimer
All the Internet addresses (URLs) given in this book were
valid at the time of going to press. However, due to the
dynamic nature of the Internet, some addresses may have
changed, or sites may have changed or ceased to exist since
publication. While the author and publishers regret any
inconvenience this may cause readers, no responsibility for
any such changes can be accepted by either the author
or the publishers.

Contents

Any words appearing in the text in bold, **like this,** are explained in the glossary. You can also look out for them in the Word Bank at the bottom of each page.

Black Death

The "Black Death" spread to Florence in 1348. It is a dreadful disease or **"plague"**. The Black Death killed half of the city's population.

You wake up in a hotel room. The room has a high ceiling and the floor is covered in tiles. It's a hot June day. The tiles feel nice and cool under your feet. Where are you?

You leave the hotel to look around. Something odd is going on at the end of the street. It looks like a crazy game of football. The players are wearing what looks like 16th-century costumes.

► Some of the tackles in Florence's *Gioco di Calcio Storico* can get quite rough.

WORD BANK   plague disease that spreads quickly and affects a lot of people

You wander up to the watching crowd. Someone explains that this game is called the *Gioco di Calcio Storico*. This is an ancient type of football game. Teams from the four quarters of the city play one another. These matches are part of a festival.

But which city are you in? "Florence – the most beautiful city in Italy!" says one of the spectators.

The duomo

Florence's most famous landmark is the *duomo* or cathedral. The Cathedral of Florence was planned in 1294. At that time nobody knew how its dome could be built. The dome was not completed until 1436.

Filippo Brunelleschi was the man who completed the Cathedral of Florence. A competition was held in 1418 to find the best design for a new dome. Brunelleschi's design won him the job.

Regions of Italy

Italy fact file

POPULATION:
57.4 million

AREA:
301,245 square kilometres
(116,311 square miles)

LANGUAGE:
Italian

CURRENCY:
Euro.

Back at your hotel, you find a map and some photos. They must have been left behind by another traveller. Whoever it was has made some notes about the different areas of Italy.

Southern Italy is hotter and drier than the north. Some of Italy's poorest regions are in the south. Many people work on small farms and earn very little money.

Market stalls selling fresh fruit and vegetables can be found on every street corner in Italy.

Italy is famous for its fashionable clothes and top fashion designers. Milan Fashion Week is a time for showing off the latest designs.

Northern Italy is the wealthiest part of Italy. Some of the country's greatest cities are here. The northern regions are famous for their great food.

Central Italy is known for its beautiful countryside. The Tuscany region is one of the prettiest areas. Some of the small towns here are among the oldest and most beautiful in Italy.

AUSTRIA

SWITZERLAND

DOLOMITE MOUNTAINS

A L P S

SLOVENIA

Lake Como

Mount Bianco

Mount Rosa

Milan

Po river

Venice

CROATIA

Turin

BOSNIA-HERZEGOVINA

FRANCE

Bologna

Arno river

Florence

Pisa

Tuscany

Siena

Tiber river

ADRIATIC SEA

A P E N N I N E   M O U N T A I N S

SERBIA

The famous city of Naples in the south attracts lots of visitors. Southern beauty spots such as the Amalfi Coast, are also popular with holidaymakers.

Rome

This is the heel

Naples

Pompeii

SARDINIA

Herculaneum

Mount Vesuvius

Mount Vesuvius

Cagliari

TYRRHENIAN SEA

This is the toe

This is called the "boot" of Italy!

Palermo

SICILY

The island of Sicily is closer to Africa than to any other European country. Sicily's buildings and cooking are a mix of North African and European styles.

FAVIGNANA

Mount Etna

Agrigento

MEDITERRANEAN SEA

ALGERIA

N
W — E
S

TUNISIA

0   300 km

0   200 miles

History of Italy

Florence

You are here!

ROME

N
W—E
S

0   150 km
0   100 miles

The city of Florence was founded in 59 BC. That was about 2,070 years ago. Its founder was the great Roman general, Julius Caesar. Caesar later became ruler of Rome and all the lands that Rome controlled.

Rome already controlled many countries. Under Caesar's leadership, the Roman armies conquered more countries. Caesar made Rome's **empire** bigger.

A group of Roman politicians stabbed Julius Caesar to death in 44 BC. They feared Caesar would make himself king of Rome.

➤

WORD BANK   empire group of countries controlled by another country

Caesar grew very powerful. At this time, Rome was a **republic**. This meant that Romans chose their own leaders. Other politicians worried that Caesar would make himself king of Rome. A king could pass on power to whoever he liked. In 44 BC, more than 2,050 years ago, Caesar was murdered.

The Roman Empire finally ended in AD 476. Even today, there are lots of reminders of the Roman Empire. People still copy the Roman style of building. Many words we use come from the Roman language called Latin.

Renaissance

In 14th century Italy, people became interested again in the ideas of ancient Greece and Rome. People began to use these ideas in their art, buildings, and writing. This was the start of a period called the Renaissance, meaning "rebirth". The Renaissance spread all around Europe. It lasted about 200 years.

The US White House was completed in 1800. It is a mix of ideas from ancient Greece and Rome. This is known as Renaissance style.

republic system of government where citizens elect people to represent them

Santa Croce

You are staying in the Santa Croce district of Florence. Santa Croce is famous for big public events. The powerful Medici family ruled Florence for many years. The Medici used Santa Croce Palace for great celebrations.

The Vatican

The Vatican City in Rome is the headquarters of the Roman Catholic religion. The Vatican is the world's smallest country. It has its own army, called the Swiss Guard.

The Medici family ruled Florence for hundreds of years. **Monuments** to the Medici are everywhere in the city.

WORD BANK monument important historical structure built to honour a special person or event

A divided land

At the time of the Medici, Italy was not one country. It was divided into separate areas with different rulers. Florence was a powerful city with its own laws.

A united Italy

In the 19th century, the kingdom of Sardinia joined together with parts of northern Italy. Sardinia is an island west of mainland Italy (see map, page 7). In 1861, the kingdom of Italy was formed. At that time only the cities of Rome and Venice were not part of Italy.

The Red Shirts

In 1860 Giuseppe Garibaldi led a thousand men from northern Italy to Sicily. Sicily is an island south of the mainland (see map, page 7). Garibaldi's men were called the Red Shirts. They captured Sicily from its French rulers. Sicily then joined the new country of Italy. Garibaldi went on to capture southern Italy.

Garibaldi leads the Red Shirts ashore at Sicily in 1860. The Red Shirts got their name because they always wore red shirts.

Landscape of Italy

The Apennine Mountains rise up behind Florence. They run almost the whole length of the country. Because of this, the Apennines are sometimes called the "spine of Italy".

Northern mountains

In the north are the Alps and the Dolomites. These mountains are higher than the Apennines (see map page 7). In the north-west, Mount Bianco stands on the border with France. Mount Bianco is Europe's highest peak.

The Tiber River flows under many ancient bridges in Rome. The dome in the background is St Peter's **Basilica** in the Vatican City.

The northern mountains are popular with skiers and snowboarders in winter.

WORD BANK basilica type of Christian church based on the design of ancient Roman halls

Rivers

Waters from the Alps, Dolomites, and northern Apennines flow into the Po River. The Po is Italy's longest river. Its valley has very good farming land.

A river flows by your hotel. This is the Arno River. The Arno Valley is famous for its vineyards and olive groves. The Tiber River rises not far from the Arno. The Tiber flows through Rome.

The weather is very dry in the south. This means that the rivers here are quite small. Some dry up completely during the hottest weather.

A volcanic land

Mount Etna in Sicily (see below) is one of the world's largest volcanoes. It is still dangerous. In 1979, nine people died on the edge of the main **crater**. A crater is the hole inside the top of a volcano.

St Peter's Basilica

Weather in Italy

You wonder what the weather is like around Italy. You want to know if you need different clothes to visit different areas.

Weather in the north

In June northern Italy is usually hot and dry. The region stays warm until September. Winters can be cold with temperatures of 5–6 °C (41–42.8 °F). There are also plenty of rainy days. The **plains,** or flat areas, sometimes get freezing winds.

Open for business

Most shops and businesses in Italy open at 9 a.m. They then close during the hottest part of the day. This is from about 1 p.m. until 4 p.m. Everything opens again until about 7:30 p.m. Most places close on Sundays.

Even during winter, the weather in Sicily is warm. This is Taormina in Sicily. It is one of Italy's smartest resorts.

SALVATAGGIO

WORD BANK   plain   high, flat area of land

Southern weather

Summers in southern Italy are similar to summers in the north. Temperatures in the south drop during winter. But they do not drop as much as in the north. Even in winter, rain and cold weather are unlikely in the south.

In the south, only the highest mountain peaks ever get snow. The northern mountains, however, get lots of snow in winter.

This table shows the different average temperatures across Italy. Look at the map on page 7 to see where these cities are located in Italy.

City:	July temp.	January temp.
Bologna	26.0 °C / 79 °F	2.5 °C / 36.5 °F
Florence	25.0 °C / 77 °F	5.6 °C / 42.8 °F
Milan	24.8 °C / 76 °F	1.9 °C / 35.4 °F
Palermo	25.3 °C / 77.5 °F	10.3 °C / 50.5 °F
Rome	25.7 °C / 78.2 °F	7.4 °C / 45.3 °F

Northern Italy gets plenty of rainfall, even in the warmer months. This picture shows St Mark's Square in the northern city of Venice.

You are feeling hungry now. You wonder what you might eat. Italy's different regions are very proud of their own styles of cooking. There are also plenty of dishes popular throughout the country.

Snacks

At lunchtime, Italians often pick up *panini* (sandwiches) or slices of hot pizza. You try some pizza. The pizza seller says he is from Naples in the south. Naples is where pizza first came from.

Pizza is a favourite Italian food. Today, it is enjoyed all around the world.

Eating out

For a bigger meal you would go to a *trattoria*.
A *trattoria* usually opens for lunch and dinner.
A *ristorante* (restaurant) only opens for dinner.

Eating together

Italian families love eating together at home.
They often spend hours preparing the food for
family get-togethers. These meals can last a long
time. They might have four or more courses.

"Fat Bologna"

Bologna is famous
throughout Italy
for its fine food.
Bolognese sauce is
now famous around
the world. In
Bologna, however,
it is called *ragu*.

Italy's warm climate is perfect for eating outside.

Out and about

After walking about in the heat and eating lunch, you are feeling sleepy. Why not take a nap? Almost everyone else will be having one.

When you wake up it is early evening. Florentines are now thinking about the *passeggiata* (stroll). All over Italy, people go out in the evening for a stroll along the main street.

Scooter crazy

Italy must be the scooter capital of the world! Scooters are a great way to get around the crowded, narrow streets of many Italian cities.

▲ Italy is the home of Vespa. Vespa is the world's most famous maker of scooters.

passeggiata traditional evening stroll along the main street

The *passeggiata* is a great way to see and chat to friends. It is also a chance to find out what is going on in your village or town.

Clothes and fashion

People also use the *passeggiata* to show off their latest clothes. Many Italians take a lot of pride in the way they dress. They are known for being fashionably dressed.

People of all ages meet up during the evening *passeggiata*.

Festivals

Italy is a **Catholic** country. The headquarters of the Roman Catholic religion is in Rome. Italy has many religious festivals. These are often in honour of particular saints.

Festivals usually start with a group of people marching in a **procession** (parade). This is followed by a religious service. Then there is celebration. There is usually music, dancing, food, and drink.

The Siena Palio

The city of Siena is just a short drive away from Florence. Every year riders and horses from all districts of Siena race around the city's central square. These famous races are called the *Palio*.

> The *Palio* is one of the world's most dangerous horse races. Riders ride without saddles.

WORD BANK fungus (plural: fungi) organism that spreads over matter and absorbs it. Types of fungi include moulds and mushrooms.

Pilgrimages

Many religious Italians take part in **pilgrimages**. These are religious journeys. They sometimes involve days of walking or a tough climb to visit a particular shrine. A shrine is a **holy** place.

Non-religious festivals

Not all Italy's festivals are religious. Some celebrate local history or local food. Others are linked to music, art, or film. For example, film-makers from around the world gather each year in Venice. They go there to show their films at the Venice film festival.

Truffle festival

The city of Alba in north-west Italy holds a **truffle** festival every October. Truffles are edible **fungi** that grow underground or around the roots of trees. A fungus is a plant-like growth such as a mushroom or mould. During this festival, people dress in **medieval** costumes (see left) and take part in parades.

medieval belonging to the period between about AD 500 and 1500

Living in Italy

Holiday fact file

These are the days when almost everyone in Italy takes a day off:

1 JANUARY – New Year's Day

6 JANUARY – Epiphany (Christian festival)

EASTER MONDAY – (Christian festival)

25 APRIL – Liberation Day (celebrates Italy's freedom from German control near the end of World War II in 1945).

Football is Italy's most popular sport. The football season starts in August. It carries on every Sunday afternoon until May.

The big-city teams have strong support from their fans. Matches between two teams from the same area cause lots of excitement. Matches between AC Milan and Inter Milan, or Roma and Lazio (both from Rome) are always important.

Sunday afternoon matches between Italy's top football teams are always colourful!

Road racing

When the football season ends, Italians turn their attention to cycling. The most important cycling event is the *Giro D'Italia*. This is a race around the country. Motor racing is another popular spectator sport. The Italian Ferrari team have very devoted fans.

Theatre and cinema

Italians also love going to the theatre and cinema in their free time. This is often a good time to enjoy a meal out as well.

More holidays

1 MAY – Labour Day

15 AUGUST – Feast of the Assumption, (Christian festival)

1 NOVEMBER – All Saints Day (Christian festival)

8 DECEMBER – Feast of the Immaculate Conception (Christian festival)

25 AND 26 DECEMBER – Christmas Day and Boxing Day (Christian festival).

Mario Cipollini (right), crosses the finish in the *Giro d'Italia*. Cipollini is one of the most successful Italian cyclists ever.

Languages

School lessons are normally in Italian. But Italian is not the main language in some regions. Schools in these areas can teach lessons in other languages:

- Trentino-Alto Adige, in the north-east – German
- Aosta Valley, in the north-west – French
- Trieste and Gorizia in the north-east – Slovene.

School

While you are here, you don't have to go to school. But what about Italian children? What is school like for them?

Italian children have to go to school between the ages of six and fifteen. The government plans to increase this to eighteen.

In the past, school used to stop for two hours in the middle of the day. Children then went home for lunch. Today, more parents are out at work. Children can now stay at school for lunch.

> Schoolchildren in Italy do not usually have to wear a uniform.

urban to do with a city or a town

Work

Most Italians live in cities and towns. They go there because this is where most jobs are based. They enjoy the restaurants and theatres. They also enjoy the sports centres and other attractions of city life.

In the countryside, some people work on farms. There are fewer farming jobs than there used to be. Today, machines often do work that people used to do.

City-dwellers

Just over 67 percent of Italians lived in **urban** areas (cities or towns) in the year 2000. This is quite low compared to some other wealthy countries. In the UK, 89 percent of people lived in urban areas. In the United States, the figure was 77 percent.

This woman is working at the Fiat car factory. It is in the north-western city of Turin. Fiat is one of Italy's biggest employers.

Life in the cities

You are here!

● ROME

N
W — E
S

0   150 km
0   100 miles

It's time to explore Italy's capital, Rome. You arrive by train at the *Stazione Termini*. This train station is in the heart of the city.

The first thing you do is to take a walk up the Esquiline Hill. From here you see the Tiber River winding through the city. In the distance you see the Vatican City. This is the centre of the Roman Catholic religion (see page 10).

Rome fact file

FOUNDED:
753 BC

POPULATION:
4 million

SEVEN HILLS OF ANCIENT ROME:
Aventine, Caelian, Capitoline, Esquiline, Palatine, Quirinal, and Viminal.

Ancient Rome was laid out around seven hills. Today's Rome is much bigger. There are now about twenty hills within the city.

▼

Ancient city

Everywhere in Rome there are ancient buildings. Many date from the time when Rome was the centre of the powerful Roman **Empire**.

The most impressive building of all is the Colosseum. This is where the rulers of ancient Rome held games to entertain the people. Trained fighters called **gladiators** took part in some games. Gladiators would fight each other until one died.

Catacombs

Catacombs are underground burial tunnels. Under Roman law, places of burial were **holy** and could not be attacked. Because of this, Christians used the catacombs to hide from their enemies.

The Colosseum is one of Rome's most famous sights. In ancient times, crowds of up to 50,000 would pack inside to watch games.

gladiator man who was forced to fight in public contests in ancient Rome

Italian cities

Rome today is a busy, crowded city. Pavements are lined with shops and cafés. People stop off for a quick coffee or pastry on their way to work.

You are enjoying exploring Rome. Florence was a fascinating place to visit too. You wonder what Italy's other big cities are like. You look back at the notes you found earlier.

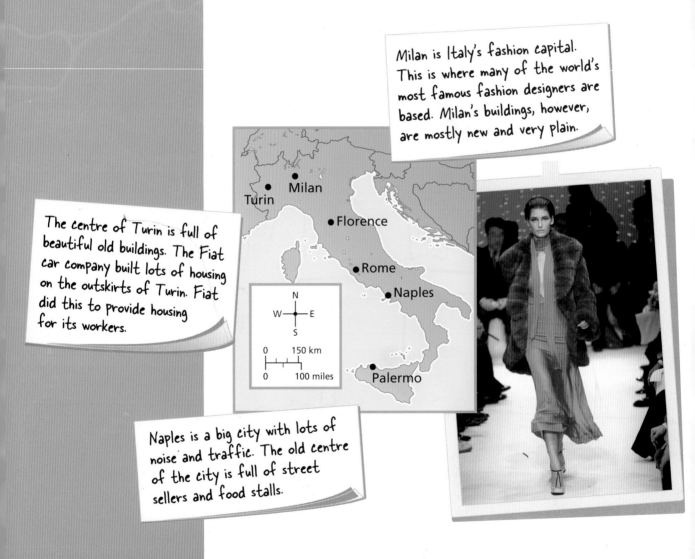

Milan is Italy's fashion capital. This is where many of the world's most famous fashion designers are based. Milan's buildings, however, are mostly new and very plain.

The centre of Turin is full of beautiful old buildings. The Fiat car company built lots of housing on the outskirts of Turin. Fiat did this to provide housing for its workers.

Naples is a big city with lots of noise and traffic. The old centre of the city is full of street sellers and food stalls.

Cagliari is on the island of Sardinia (see map on page 7). The city has a rich history and blue skies all year. African and European styles blend together in Palermo. It is in Sicily (see map, page 28).

Then there are the mainland cities. You look at your guide book to find out about them.

The first capital

The country of Italy was formed in 1861. At first, Turin was Italy's capital. This was where Italy's first king, Victor Emmanuel II, was born. Ten years later, however, Rome became the new capital.

South of Naples, the beautiful Amalfi Coast is popular with holidaymakers from all over Europe.

Problems in Rome

The first thing you notice about Rome is the ancient buildings. The next thing you notice is the traffic! The streets are clogged with cars. Drivers honk their horns and scooters zip between the cars.

Rome's traffic problems are causing **pollution**. This pollution is damaging the ancient **monuments**. The Colosseum is one of the monuments or historic buildings that has been damaged in this way. Pollution eats away at the stone they are built from.

In Italy, everyone seems to have a car. This can lead to some very busy roads.

WORD BANK   pollution release of harmful chemicals or waste into the air, water, or soil

Problems in other cities

Other Italian cities also have traffic problems. Few, however, are as bad as Rome's. There is also a shortage of homes in many cities. People sometimes have to live crowded together.

There are some areas of poverty around the edges of the cities. People in these parts struggle to earn enough money to live on.

The city of Venice is built on more than 100 small islands. Between the islands there are canals and bridges. There are no cars in Venice's historic centre.

monument important historical structure built to honour a special person or event

Road and rail

Many Italian cities have traffic problems. The main roads linking Italy's cities, however, are often excellent.

The trains that run between the cities are usually very good. High-speed trains also link Italian cities with cities in other European countries. Slower, local trains run to the smaller towns and villages.

Water-buses

Water-buses

In Venice, people catch *vaporetti* (water-buses) instead of ordinary buses. These boats stop at docks all over the city. *Vaporetti* are the easiest way to get about (see picture below).

A high-speed train whizzes through the beautiful countryside of Tuscany.

Planes

Most international flights run from Italy's big cities, such as Milan, Rome, or Pisa.

Airports in Italy's smaller cities and towns are getting busier, however. Airlines that offer cheap flights often use these smaller airports. This is because it costs more to use the bigger airports.

Amalfi Coast

One of the most famous roads in Italy winds along the Amalfi Coast. This is a stretch of the western coast, south of Naples. Every weekend it is busy with people racing along in flashy cars or fast motorbikes.

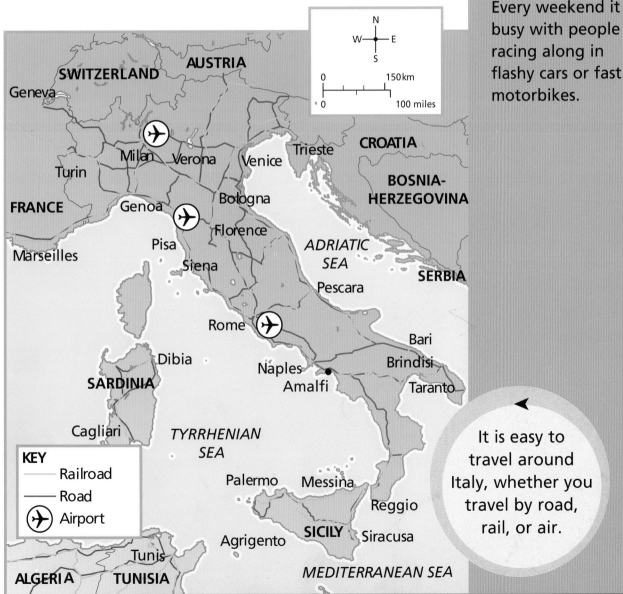

KEY
- Railroad
- Road
- ✈ Airport

It is easy to travel around Italy, whether you travel by road, rail, or air.

Rome has some big outdoor markets. You wander into one of them. There are stalls selling fish, meat, cheese, fruit and vegetables, cakes, and bread. A lot of this food comes from the Italian countryside.

Farming in Italy

Many Italian farms are small. They are some of the smallest farms in Europe. The big farms are usually on the **plains** through which rivers flow. The Po **Valley** in the north has rich farmland and large farms.

Cooperatives

Groups of small farmers often join together to form a **cooperative**. This is an organization owned by the people who work in it. Everyone in the cooperative shares any costs. For example, they share the cost of transporting crops to market.

Hilly areas like Tuscany and Umbria in central Italy are full of small farms. Some of them have beautiful old buildings.

WORD BANK cooperative organization that is owned by everyone who works within it

Food for export

Italian food is popular all around the world. Italian olive oil, sun-dried tomatoes, and dried porcini mushrooms are **exported**, or sold abroad. Pasta is one of the world's favourite Italian foods. A lot of the pasta in shops back home is made in Italy.

Italian pasta comes in hundreds of different shapes, sizes, and colours.

export to sell a country's produce abroad

The south

Life in the south has often been hard for small farmers. In the past, a farmer's land could be a long walk from his home. It could also be a long way from a water supply. The poor soil in parts of the south made it difficult to grow crops.

Even today, many southern farmers have very small plots of land. These farmers find it hard to make a good living from farming.

Mafia

The Mafia is an organization that began in the Sicilian countryside. Local chiefs controlled water wells. They made people pay to use these wells. People who did not pay were often harshly punished. By the 1950s, the Mafia had grown into an international crime organization.

Calabria in the south is one of Italy's poorest regions. People still use donkeys and carts to get around.

WORD BANK   second home house that is not the owner's main home

New arrivals

People from other parts of Europe are buying houses in the northern Italian countryside. Some make their homes in Italy. Others buy houses as **second homes**. This means they do not live in them all the time.

Price rises

These wealthy foreign buyers create jobs for local people. Unfortunately, they have also caused house prices to rise. This means that young local people often cannot afford to buy their own homes.

The village of Fora d'Agra is in the hills of Sicily. In the past, people who lived in hilltop villages like this had a long walk each day to get to their fields.

Fish-loving Italians

As you wander around the market in Rome you see many different kinds of fish for sale. There are slippery eels, garfish with pointy noses, and octopus.

Italians love eating fish. Italy has a long coastline with plenty of fishing ports. The demand for fish is so great, however, that Italy has to buy fish from other countries.

This market in Rome **specializes** in selling all types of fish and seafood.

WORD BANK   **specialize** to be concerned with just one particular type of product or area of work

Shellfish are very popular. Shellfish such as mussels, shrimps, or prawns are on the menus in most Italian restaurants.

Some of the fish you see at the market are freshwater fish, such as trout. Freshwater fish come from lakes and rivers. Most fish, however, will come from the sea.

Fishing for tuna

Favignana is an island close to Sicily. On Favignana, the fisherman trap tuna in a giant circular net. The fishermen then spear these huge fish on hooks attached to long poles. This method of killing tuna is known as the *mattanza*.

Some people say the *mattanza* is cruel. Others claim that it is probably less cruel than using a hook and line or ordinary nets.

La Befana

La Befana was a good witch from long ago who loved children. Legend says she wanders around Italy on 5 January leaving presents for children. Rome holds a toy fair on 6 January in her honour.

Tourism and travel

On your last day in Rome, you study a guidebook on Italy. You make notes about the different places in Italy you haven't visited yet.

The city of Siena in central Italy (see map, right) is said to be one of the most beautiful towns in Italy. The historic centre is home to the Palio horse race (see page 20).

Pisa in central Italy (see map, right) is home to one of Italy's most famous sights. The Leaning Tower of Pisa was built on sandy soil. This has caused the tower to lean over slowly through the years. Now the Tower leans dramatically.

Pompeii and Herculaneum — these were two ancient Roman towns. They were destroyed in AD 79 when the volcano Mount Vesuvius, near Naples (see map, above), **erupted**. Today, visitors come to see the remains of the towns.

erupt to release lava and ash. This happens when a volcano becomes active.

There are more canals and boats in Venice (see map, page 40) than roads and cars. It is a very beautiful city. Try to pick a quiet time to visit. Up to 15 million tourists go there every year.

Before the days of the Roman Empire, the Greeks ruled parts of Sicily and southern Italy. There are Greek temples at Agrigento in Sicily (see map, page 40) that were built about 2,300 years ago.

Stay, or go home?

So, you've been to Rome and Florence. You've also seen the Tuscan countryside between the two cities. There is still lots to do though. Here are some activities you might like to try.

Via ferrata

Via ferrata routes are in the Dolomite Mountains (see map, page 7). These routes combine walking and climbing. Sometimes they take you up iron ladders bolted to the rockface.

Via ferrata means "iron road". People in search of adventure come to the Dolomite Mountains to climb these steep iron ladders.

Snowboard Sestriere

You could try snowboarding at Sestriere. This is one of Italy's top ski resorts. It is located in the Alps, near Turin.

Climb Mount Etna

Mount Etna in Sicily is one of the world's largest volcanoes. You can walk right up to the main crater (see right).

Surf Sardinia

The west coast of Sardinia is one of the best places in the Mediterranean for surfing.

Windsurf on Lake Como

Beautiful Lake Como in the north is a favourite spot for windsurfers. Winds from the mountains blow across the lake.

➤ Italy's northern lakes are home to some of Europe's best inland windsurfing.

Find out more

You can find out more about Italy using the books, websites, and addresses listed below:

World Wide Web

If you want to find out more about Italy, you can search the Internet using keywords such as these:

- Italy
- Colosseum
- Mount Etna

You can also find your own keywords by using words from this book. Try using a search directory such as **yahooligans.com**.

Movies

Roman Holiday (1953)
One of the most famous films to be set in Rome.

The Italian Job (1969)
A gang of robbers tries to steal a load of gold from Turin.

The Italian Embassy

The Italian **Embassy** in your own country has lots of information about Italy. The UK embassy address is:

Italian Embassy in London
14, Three Kings Yard
Davies Street
London W1K 2EH.

You can find details of other Italian embassies and more information about Italy on the following website:

www.italy.embassyhomepage.com

Further reading

The following books are packed with useful information about Italy:

Countries of the World: Italy, Sally Garrington (Facts on File, 2004)

Take Your Camera: Italy, Ted Park (Raintree, 2004)

The Rough Guide To Italy, Martin Dunford (Rough Guides, 2005)

republic system of government where citizens elect people to represent them

Timeline

753 BC
According to legend, Romulus and Remus founded the city of Rome.

509 BC
Rome becomes a **republic**.

264–146 BC
Rome takes control of more overseas lands during the Punic Wars.

59 BC
Florence founded.

44 BC
Caesar murdered.

27 BC
Augustus becomes Rome's first emperor.

79 AD
Pompeii and Herculaneum destroyed when Mount Vesuvius erupts.

96–180 AD
The Roman Empire is at its most powerful.

395
The Roman Empire splits into two parts, the West and East Roman Empire.

476
The last emperor of the West Roman Empire is overthrown.

962
Otto the Great is crowned emperor. This marks the start of what was later called the Holy Roman Empire.

1519
King Charles I of Spain becomes emperor of the Holy Roman Empire.

1796
Napoleon Bonaparte conquers Italy for France.

1814–1815
Napoleon is defeated. Italy is returned to its rulers.

1861
The Kingdom of Italy is formed.

1870
Rome becomes part of Italy.

1871
Rome becomes Italy's capital city.

1915–1918
Italy fights on the same side as France, Russia, Britain, and the United States in World War I.

1922
Benito Mussolini becomes prime minister.

1940–1943
Italy fights on Germany's side in World War II.

1943
Italy surrenders to the **Allies**.

1946
The Republic of Italy is established.

1980
An earthquake strikes southern Italy killing over 4,500 people.

Italy – facts and figures

Italy's flag was first used in 1796. Italy was then part of the French **Empire**. Napoleon Bonaparte was leader of France and Italy. He designed the Italian flag to look like the French Flag. He changed the French blue to green because it was his favourite colour.

People and places

- Population: 57.4 million.
- Average life expectancy: 78.2 years.

What's in a name?

- Italy's name comes from the ancient Roman word *Italia*. *Italia* meant "land of oxen" or "grazing land". Italy's official name is *Repubblica Italiana*.

Money matters

- Italy's currency is the Euro. Before the Euro, the currency was the lira.
- Average annual earnings: Men – £18,230 (US$33,084) Women – £8,142 (US$14,719).

Food facts

- The ice-cream cone was invented by Italians.
- The national dish is pasta. The average Italian is said to eat a whopping 25 kilograms (55 pounds) of pasta a year.

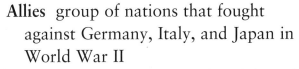

Allies group of nations that fought against Germany, Italy, and Japan in World War II

basilica type of Christian church based on the design of ancient Roman halls

catacombs tunnels used as burial chambers

Catholic to do with the Roman Catholic religion, or a follower of the Roman Catholic religion

cooperative organization that is owned by everyone who works within it

crater funnel-shaped hole inside the top of a volcano

embassy place where another country has an official building

empire group of countries controlled by another country

erupt to release lava and ash. This happens when a volcano becomes active.

export to sell a country's produce abroad

fungus (plural: fungi) organism that spreads over matter and absorbs it. Types of fungi include moulds and mushrooms.

gladiator man who was forced to fight in public contests in ancient Rome

holy associated with a divine power

medieval belonging to the period between about AD 500 and 1500

monument important historical structure built to honour a special person or event

passeggiata traditional evening stroll along the main street

pilgrimage journey that a person makes to a holy place

plague disease that spreads quickly and affects a lot of people

plain high, flat area of land

pollution release of harmful chemicals or waste into the air, water, or soil

procession group of people marching in a ceremony

republic system of government where citizens elect people to represent them

second home house that is not the owner's main home

specialize to be concerned with just one particular type of product or area of work

truffle very tasty underground fungus, a bit like a mushroom

urban to do with a city or a town

valley area of lowland between ranges of hills or mountains

Index

Titles in the *Destination Detectives* series include:

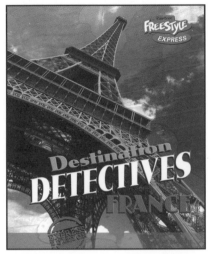

Hardback   1 406 20400 5

Hardback   1 406 20401 3

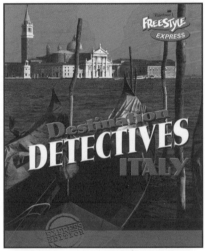

Hardback   1 406 20402 1

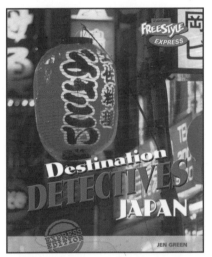

Hardback   1 406 20403 X

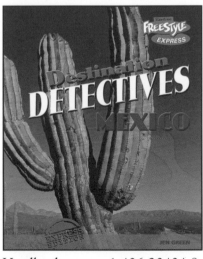

Hardback   1 406 20404 8

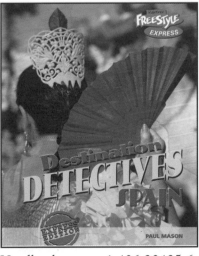

Hardback   1 406 20405 6

Find out about the other titles in this series on our website www.raintreepublishers.co.uk